Currently, On Purpose

A book of poems
by Callan Handmaker

Currently on Purpose was self-published in the United States
as a product of Ubelong on February Fourteenth, Twenty Nineteen

Happy Valentine's Day to all the broken hearts out there </3

Find more at ubelongherenow.com

ISBN: 9781796243758
Printed in the United States of America

Hi, I'm Callan.

Welcome to *Currently on Purpose,* where u get to peek inside my head for a brisk 29 poems. This is a book about finding your self through embracing your self. This is a book about love, possibility, and feeling, where u will read about struggle, life-questions, and longing. This is a book about a universal story in which I hope u can find yourself as a character, because this – is a book for u.

Thank u for being on this journey with me.

Transparently,
Callan <3

Steps on the Journey

07..Child
09..Emotions
11...To
13...They Said
15..Separate
17...I Don't Know U Yet
19..Dream
21..Nosebleeds
23..Sleeves
25...Desperate
27..Across the Street
29...Dear TBD
31...Honest in the Sky
33..Softer
35...Call Me Crazy
37...Be Misunderstood
39...Too
41..What is Love
43..If U Feel it
45..Your Way
47..Nobody
49..Sober
51..My Microphone
53..Maybe
55..Love I Fear
57..Confiding in U
59..Love & Drugs
61...Currently on Purpose
63...Nothing is Perfect

Child

The other day I met myself as a child

He was without a care, feeling so wild

So, I sat him down, said take a second and breathe

Everything will be okay one day, U better believe

So just stop counting sheep

Fall asleep

and be free

All your demons will leave and u will light up the streets

But, please

Don't follow me

'Cause who am I to see

I'm just another man – not the one U should be

Emotions

When I was little

I got made fun of for having emotions

When I got older

I got in trouble at work for having emotions

I keep myself up at night because I have emotions

I've lost friends because I care too much.

To

Speak to stay honest;

Act to show conviction;

Forgive to welcome progress;

& Connect to draw chance.

But when u feel – just feel.

They Said

"Don't say that," they said.

"Don't do it like that," they said.

"Ask permission," they said.

"If I were u…" they said.

But you're not.

Separate

Separate

Separate from what u think u know

Separate

Separate from the stories u tell your self

Separate

Separate from the vines in your life

Separate

Separate from the things that are not real

Separate

Separate from your demons

Separate from your angels

Separate

I Don't Know U Yet

All I need is some love and affection

Wish all I want could be real in a second

U need a story? Use my life as a reference

U want a friend? Give a call or a beckon

I love u so much – but I don't know u yet

All I know is that I'm gonna regret

If I don't find u by the time that I'm dead

I'd'a lost all my purpose, or maybe even my head

When I find the right time in the right mind, yea I'll know it

If you're gonna be mine, I'll be just fine and I'll show it

So don't be shy, just give a try and we'll grow it

Give me a chance, and I promise I won't blow it

Dream

Joke, so u don't take yourself too seriously.

Love, to open your heart to possibility.

Fall, to feel yourself rise again – but

Dream, because otherwise u are just asleep.

Nosebleeds

The tickets are the cheapest in the nosebleeds

They don't charge for what u can see

They don't charge for what u can hear

They don't realize the detail u can find when u are up in the nosebleeds

They don't realize how being far away, can show u the most love

The tickets are the cheapest in the nosebleeds

They don't charge for what u can feel

They don't charge for what u can understand

They don't realize the extra senses u may gain when u are up in the nosebleeds

They don't realize that when u are up so high

So high that coming back down

Feels like the biggest journey

U may ever

– have to encounter –

Causes u to fall

To fall harder than u have ever fallen before

The tickets are the cheapest in the nosebleeds

They don't charge for what u can see

They don't charge for what u can feel

Because they can't put a price on love

They can't put a price on heartbreak

Sleeves

Sometimes I wish I didn't wear my emotions on my sleeve.

I wonder what that would feel like.

A close friend once told me that otherwise I wouldn't be who I am.

I guess they're right.

Desperate

I try not to fuxk it up by being myself

Turns out I fuxk it up by not being myself

They tell me it's always this, never that

Say it's never me, always them

Call me just a friend.

But if it's never me

Then why is everyone so happy

If it's meant to be

Then I guess I'm meant to be lonely

But someone told me

A sign if u are lonely

That u are in desperate need of your self

Across the Street

Find yourself a new home

Find yourself a new place to stay at night

Not a real place, but a place inside your head

And as u look out the window into the dark

U can see your mind chattering as the lights flicker

Across the street

Be there

Be there for that neighbor

Dear TBD

What u make me feel I can't forget
So I write down
I can't let it slip
So it has to be right now

Today it is simple:
I need u in my life now
I need u in my life
Yea, I need u in my life now

Let's runaway today
No better time than right now
I don't know much
Except I need u in my life now

It's very nice to meet u
We'll get acquainted on the ride down
But all I know is right now
That's all I can write down

Everything I do just seems never good enough
While everything u do is always more than good enough
Maybe one day I will be good enough
Maybe tomorrow I will feel good enough

Because what does it really mean to be at a 10?
On a scale of one to in-love I'm here 'til the end
Look at me I'm serious I don't need to pretend
Is something on your mind? U can feel free to vent

If when u meet the 1 u hear bells and nice sounds
Then a 10-string symphony is what I hear right now
Like when u are young u find the best slide to slide down
I need u in my life, yea I need u in my life now

At the end of the day I hope u need me too
And I'll live my days as u need me to
Whatever it takes, I will see this through
'Cause I won't be okay unless it's me and u

Honest in the Sky

They say the ones that aren't lost

Are the most lost of all

The ones who don't love

Are the least loved of all

The ones who don't grow

Are the ones who won't evolve

And the ones who say no

Don't get yesses at all

Because it works like that

Yea the worst is that:

U never realize 'til it's too late to go back

& What if? Your real friends aren't real

U gotta ask others just to know how U feel

When was the last time that

U sat down and just felt

What's really going on and

Tried to let it all melt

Stop freezing up and closing off

U may find when u open up

The flowers start to bloom and everything begins to flow enough

So that u can finally breathe and ask why

Look up

The clouds spell honest in the sky

Softer

Catch me writing stories in my head

Almost like an author

Catch me doing things I shouldn't

Just like my father

Sometimes I need a little love that I wish u would offer

Find myself feeling tough but always acting softer

Yea they tell me it's not personal

But it's personal

Everyone playing dramas, just like they're at rehearsal

Rolling tapes back in my head, I think it's in reverse now

I can't escape this, praying, feels like I'm in a church now

The ones that seem to find me are the ones to leave behind me

Because I attract the ones that seem to need me

Then say goodbye to me

Call Me Crazy

Call me crazy.

Call me unreasonable

Call me anxious

Call me funny

Call me sad

Call me weird

Call me irreplaceable

Call me paranoid

Call me annoying

Call me loving

Call me arrogant

Call me rude

Call me genuine

Call me crazy.

Be Misunderstood

Have u stopped to notice?

This moment won't come again.

Have u stopped to notice?

There are billions of people in this world.

Some are bound to be confused by u.

Have u stopped to notice?

Your raw self is powerful.

So, be misunderstood –

If it means u get to live an uncensored life.

Have u stopped to notice?

It's okay.

Sooner or later, everyone else will.

Too

Too sensitive

Too honest

Too unfiltered

Too touchy

Too silly

Too deep

Too caring

Too comfortable

Too forward

Too myself.

What is Love

What is love

Maybe a spirit or a dove

Flying above

U want it

But u just can't catch it

Something about it

What is love

What is love

Maybe a friend maybe a foe

U never know

U need it

U can't live without it

But u still fight it

What is love?

If it isn't everything to me

If U Feel It

There is a world

Where the cold is welcome and

Blankets are allowed;

Sadness is beautiful and

Struggle is strong.

If u feel it –

U will see.

If u feel it.

Your Way

They tell u when u are younger:

"Not everything will go your way."

This is true.

Or is it not?

Nobody

Sometimes I feel that everything would be easier

If there were no people in my life.

I guess I'll never know.

Sober

Sober:

A label.

Something only those who know the opposite can be stuck with.

Sober:

A one way road.

Somewhere only those who know the opposite can walk down.

Sober:

A performance.

Eternally trapped on Earth's stage playing the world's favorite matinee.

My Microphone

I just wanna let out

That if I'm gonna be loud

It's gonna be on my microphone

Out to my crowd

And if I'm not allowed

Then u may not be proud

And I'm sorry! If saying that

Might just make u frown

But I gotta do my own thing

And I want u to do your own thing

'Cause if we're not ourselves

Then who really are we being?

If not just another fake soul

That every single day brings

Maybe

Do u believe in love?

Do u believe in fear?

Do u believe in fate?

Do u believe in accidents?

Do u believe in conviction?

Do u believe in magic?

Maybe.

Or maybe, it's not too late.

Love I Fear

All the ones that like me
Are taken or they're far away
And the ones that I like
Don't like me in that way

What am I to do?
What am I to say?
Sitting on my hands
Got my mouth shut every other day

They tell me not to try
They say that it's okay
They say I gotta love myself
To find the love I crave

But it's just a cycle
Nothing I can save
Love me 'til I die
Dig me down my grave

Call me on the phone
To call me wonderful
Please write me a note
Every day you're gone

'Cause it's like I miss u
Even when you're here
Seems like the love I want
Is the love I fear

Confiding in U

Sometimes it feels like I don't know what's going on

But I wanna keep going 'til I'm all the way gone

Like everything I do is just all the way wrong

But I can't stop searching for that place I call home

Maybe one day I will find it in u

From confiding in u

Instead of blinding the truth

'Cause u know all I want is to be flying with u

This is me speaking

Instead of signing with u

Love & Drugs

Seems like I'm always just grasping at the moment

Like it's right there but I just can't hold it

Filling a void that I promise has a hole in it

The devil wanted my soul but I already sold it

Currently on Purpose

Then: I was

Later: I will

Right now: I am

Nothing is Perfect

Nothing is Perfect

isn't it Beautiful

Thank u.

Hi there – me again. I hope u enjoyed the book and that it has offered some meaning in to your current situation. If, by chance, it has left u pondering to the point that u are feeling like a chat, I want to offer myself as a resource to u now or anytime here on. Please feel free to reach out to me, personally, by emailing ubelongherenow@gmail.com with whatever may be on your mind.

Honestly,
Callan

Author, Callan Handmaker, is a meaning maker: one who chooses to believe there is a reason for each occurrence around them. As founder of Ubelong, a lifestyle brand around raw self-expression and trusting your path, Callan invites u to live "currently on purpose" with him and delve into the honest thoughts and emotions that we all may share underneath the surface. Open up. <3

Currently on Purpose is a product of Ubelong.
Find more at ubelongherenow.com

Made in the USA
Monee, IL
19 May 2022

96679021R10038